THE GOD IN YOU BIBLE STUDY SERIES

CHANGED!

REFLECTING YOUR LOVE FOR GOD

A Bible Study by

Churches Alive!

MINISTERING TO THE CHURCHES OF THE WORLD
Box 3800, San Bernardino, California 92413

Published by

NAVPRESS ◢®

A MINISTRY OF THE NAVIGATORS
P.O. BOX 35001, COLORADO SPRINGS, COLORADO 80935

Seventh printing, 1991

Cover illustration: Don Weller

Scripture quotations are from the *Holy Bible:
New International Version* (NIV). Copyright
© 1973, 1978, 1984, International Bible
Society. Used by permission of Zondervan
Bible Publishers.

Printed in the United States of America

Contents

Because we share kindred aims for helping local churches fulfill Christ's Great Commission to "go and make disciples," NavPress and Churches Alive have joined efforts on certain strategic publishing projects that are intended to bring effective disciplemaking resources into the service of the local church.

For more than a decade, Churches Alive has teamed up with churches of all denominations to establish vigorous disciplemaking ministries. At the same time, NavPress has focused on publishing Bible studies, books, and other resources that have grown out of The Navigators' 50 years of disciplemaking experience.

Now, together, we're working to offer special products like this one that are designed to stimulate a deeper, more fruitful commitment to Christ in the local gatherings of His Church.

The God in You Bible Study Series *was written by Russ Korth, Ron Wormser, Jr., and Ron Wormser, Sr. of Churches Alive. Many individuals from both Churches Alive and NavPress contributed greatly in bringing this project to publication.*

About the Author

In your hand you have just one item of a *wide range* of discipling helps, authored and developed by Churches Alive with *one overall, church-centered, biblical concept* in mind: GROWING BY DISCIPLING!

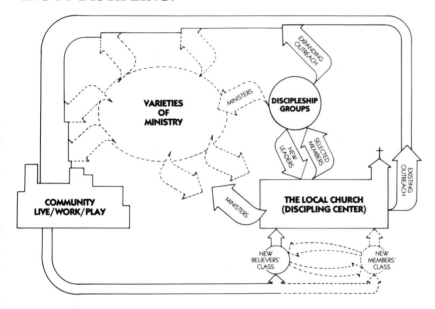

Convinced that the local church is the heart of God's plan for the world, a number of Christian leaders joined in 1973 to form Churches Alive. They saw the need for someone to work hand-in-hand with local churches to help them develop fruitful discipleship ministries.

Today, the ministry of Churches Alive has grown to include personal consulting assistance to church leaders, a variety of discipleship books and materials, and training conferences for clergy and laypeople. These methods and materials have proven effective in churches large and small of over 45 denominations.

From their commitment and experience in church ministry, Churches Alive developed the Growing by Discipling plan to help you

- minister to people at their levels of maturity.
- equip people for ministry.
- generate mature leaders.
- perpetuate quality.
- balance growth and outreach.

Every part of Growing by Discipling works together in harmony to meet the diverse needs of people—from veteran church members to the newly awakened in Christ. This discipling approach allows you to integrate present fruitful ministries and create additional ones through the new leaders you develop.

This concept follows Christ's disciplemaking example by helping you to meet people at their points of need. Then, you help them build their dependence on God so they experience His love and power. Finally, you equip them to reach out to others in a loving, effective, and balanced ministry of evangelism and helping hands.

Headquartered in San Bernardino, California, with staff across the United States and in Europe, Churches Alive continues to expand its ministry in North America and overseas.

Introduction

You are changed. You are changing.

In some areas you are changing slowly. In others, rapidly.

The changes God is making in your life begin inside, and in time, they are revealed on the outside. These changes are not the process of perfecting your acting ability. The God who is in you is expressing His nature through you.

Don't be deceived into thinking these changes all come automatically. You're going to have to work at changing. That's one reason you have God's power in you. The Apostle Paul knew who was at work in him: "By the grace of God I am what I am, and his grace to me was not without effect. No, I worked harder than all of them—yet not I, but the grace of God that was with me" (1 Corinthians 15:10).

HOW TO USE THIS BIBLE STUDY. This book leads you through a unique approach to making the Bible meaningful. In each chapter you will study one passage, not isolated verses, to explore some of the major themes of God's Word. In the process, you'll learn Bible study methods that will be useful for the rest of your life.

You will gain maximum benefit from this book by completing the questions about the study passage and then meeting with a group of people to discuss what you discovered in your study.

No doubt, your group could spend many weeks exploring the richness of just one of these Bible passages. But much greater profit accompanies a pace of one chapter each week. This stride guarantees sustained enthusiasm that will leave people wanting more.

The leader's guide designed for this series aids the group leader in launching and guiding the discussion. It provides help for using the series in a home-study group or a classroom setting.

HINTS TO ENHANCE YOUR EXPERIENCE. The translation used in writing this study is the *New International Version* (NIV) of the Bible. All quotations are from this translation.

Though written using the NIV, this workbook adapts readily to other Bible translations. In fact, it adds interest and variety in group discussions when people use different translations.

Your book includes space to answer each question. But some people choose to mark some of their answers in an inexpensive Bible. Creating a study Bible like this allows a person to benefit from notes and information year after year.

Above all, *use* the insight you gain. The truths of the Bible were not recorded to rest on dusty shelves. God designed them to live in the experiences of people. In preparing this series, the authors never intended merely to increase your intellectual knowledge of the Bible—but to help you put into action the tremendous resources available in Jesus Christ.

"Could you renew Dexter for me?"

1. Renewed

Study passage   Ephesians 4:17-32

Focus   Ephesians 4:24: Put on the new self, created to be like God in true righteousness and holiness.

1 This passage presents changing from the "old self" to a "new self." In the chart, record the characteristics of the old self and the new self, as found in Ephesians 4:17-32.

Old self	New self
Futile (verse 17)	
futile mind	*renewing ʃ of mind*

Old self	New self
vanity of mind (handwritten) darkened understanding	speak truth ē neighbor
alienated from life of God	member of ē another
ignorance	work to give
hard heart	speak to edify, give grace
callous	be kind, forgiving, tender hearts
licentious	be angry but don't sin
doing uncleaness	righteous
greed *corrupted th lust, deceit*	holy
corrupt deceived	

Even people without Christ have a moral conscience that gives them a sense of right and wrong. What do you think is the difference between a moral conscience and the new self presented in this passage?

based on desire to obey word of God (God)
to see Him as standard of rt/wrong
an absolute standard outside of self

2 The renewing process from the old self to the new self often involves a replacement of the bad with something good. Describe each replacement in these verses:

Verse 25

falsehood ē truth

Verse 28

stop stealing — work so I can give
stealing ē honest work ē hands

Verse 29

no evil talk — only edifying, fitting, imparting grace
evil talk ē edifying, fit, gracious talk
corrupt

Verses 31-32

bitterness — *kindness,*
wrath — *tender-hearted*
anger — *forgiving as Christ forgave me*
clamor
slander
malice

11

3 Using the same pattern as you did for the verses on page 11, write a replacement goal that is appropriate for your life; for example, "Instead of complaining, I should look for the good and thank God for it."

I must renew my mind c the word
+ 5:1 be an imitator of God ; become
a beloved son of God

---

4 Everyone feels angry from time to time, and no replacement is suggested for anger. Instead, the passage says, "In your anger, do not sin" (verse 26). What do you think you can do to fulfill that command?

Keep quiet Ps 4:4 Calm c my own
heart in prt

What aspects of anger do you think give the Devil a "foot-hold"? (Verse 27) *Oppressing it, causing*
a reaction + re-action

Jas 1:19-20

Use a concordance to find at least three verses in Proverbs that mention anger. Summarize their teaching.

Pr 14:29 great u   17:27 knowledge, w
15:18
16:32 greater   anger i foolish
29:20, 22   control i wise
19:11 good sense,
*   glory*
12:16 fools
Job 5:2

What do you conclude from these proverbs?

A Christian must be greater than
anger, vexation etc

renew my mind

5 In verse 23, you are commanded to have a new mind. Your thoughts and attitudes are influenced by the ideas you receive. What are some Christian and non-Christian influences that "program" people's minds today?

TV, all media
art, drama
tyranny of majority.
Church
tape.

Bible
fellowship
witness

Which of these are renewing influences for your mind?

Bible good speaker tapes / to / meeting

Which of these feed the old self?

all else

6 Seeing progress in putting off the old self and putting on the new self should encourage you. What areas of your life show you are renewed? *disappointment, sadness & sin*

What area of your life doesn't seem to be renewed? *my speech, reaction to time, travel - abrogation of my rights*

What have you learned from this study that will help you deal with this?

renew x / x / x /

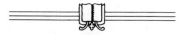

Do not conform any longer to the pattern of this world, but be transformed by the renewing of your mind. Then you will be able to test and approve what God's will is—his good, pleasing and perfect will.

Paul to the Romans
Romans 12:2

"Good news, Reverend. The board has voted to pray for your recovery. The vote was 5 to 4."

2. Loving

Study passage   1 Corinthians 13

Focus   1 Corinthians 13:13: And now these three remain: faith, hope and love. But the greatest of these is love.

1 In this passage, you will study love one to another primarily. To understand the love you should have for others, complete the two charts, referring to verses 4-7.

Love is	Love is not
patient	emulous
kind	insolent
(self effacing, meek,	rash
modest, humble	puffed up (vainglorious)
	quickly provoked

14

Love does	Love does not
rejoices ī the truth	behave in an unseemly manner
bears all things	seek its own
believes " "	impute evil
hopes " "	rejoice at iniquity
endures " "	

2 Verses 4-7 describe love, while the rest of the chapter reflects the importance of love. Without using verses 4-7, tell how the rest of the chapter presents love (for example, "Love is necessary for your actions to be meaningful"—verses 1-3).

1-3   3 love, no work is good
5 love I am nothing, can gain nothing
love is a consistent, permanent attitude
great virtues live, but love is greatest - the other
2 ⁵ love are not genuine?
love is maturity - leaving childish selfishness behind, i
Christlikeness

3 Love includes actions. But all good actions are not necessarily a result of love. Imagine you are a publicity agent for a person matching the description in verses 1-3. Write a press release describing this person's best qualities. The greatest speaker whoever lived
He speaks better than anyone, in any language - He is
the charismatic. He knows the entire Bible, & explains
for God, the future, life, everything. He does miracles
i f, for God's glory. He gave away all he had, beat his body
into submission   a charismatic mystical prophet who can do
anything -
mercy

What do you expect people to think of this person?
Many would follow, support, even worship him;
give him money, support; make him famous

What does God think of this person? (Verses 1-3)
His speaking is vain, his prophecy, miracles
He is noise ō substance, he is nothing, he can
gain nothing

4 First Corinthians 12 and 14 center on the subject of spiritual gifts. Why do you think Paul inserted this passage on love in the middle of his teaching on spiritual gifts?

gifts can lead to
arrogance
impatience
competition
envy

5 Verse 11 indicates that "childish ways" should be put away. What do you think some of these childish ways are?

self centered, calling attn to onself
in gifts. using gifts for display

6 Although love is one of the main topics of the New Testament, there are people who call themselves Christians but act very unloving. What do you consider to be the predominant reason?

_____ They don't know about love.

__✓__ They don't have power to love. *unsaved*

_____ They don't want to love.

__✓__ They are immature. *new †*

_____ Other: _____

What is your best suggestion to overcome this problem?

discipleship. get word in

7 Love evokes both spontaneous action and deliberate deeds. Describe a specific action you plan to take that shows love

to your spouse.

listen to her
be affectionate

to your family.

listen,
ask about their lives
hug the girls
what to react

to someone in your church.

to someone outside of your church.

be a friend

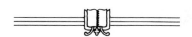

Perfect love
  Slow to suspect—quick to trust
  Slow to condemn—quick to justify
  Slow to offend—quick to defend
  Slow to expose—quick to shield
  Slow to reprimand—quick to forbear
  Slow to belittle—quick to appreciate
  Slow to demand—quick to give
  Slow to provoke—quick to conciliate
  Slow to hinder—quick to help
  Slow to resent—quick to forgive

"It's a tricky theological point. You say you covet your neighbor's humility?"

3. Humble

Study passage Philippians 2:1-11

Focus Philippians 2:3: Do nothing out of selfish ambition or vain conceit, but in humility consider others better than yourselves.

1 Paul, the author of this letter, begins this passage with four conditional phrases identified by the word *if*. Write them in the chart and give an example of one of them in your life.

Phrase	Example
If there is any encouragement in Christ	

Phrase	Example
Any incentive of love	for MG- cleaning BR
any participation in the S	accepting ad, people & hope
any affection & sympathy	

---

2 Since the conditions of verse 1 are intended for your life, what should you do? (Verses 2-4)

Take care of others; be really concerned for their welfare or let "go ahead in traffic" & invitation.

---

3 How does being humble relate to each of the following responsibilities?

Verse 3 says you should "consider others better than yourselves."

Not self centered - real humility put them in out, comfort first

Verse 5 says, "Your attitude should be the same as that of Christ Jesus."

He considered the Father better than himself, became a slave, & gave up his life.

Do you think Jesus considered others better than Himself? Explain.

He died so other could live; served his disciples, took no advantage he could have

---

4 Jesus is your example of humility. What do verses 5-8 say or imply about

what He thought about Himself?

couldn't hold on to equity c God

His attitude toward others?

service, a slave

His actions?

He gave up his life

---

5 What are some other actions that reflect Jesus' humility?

---

6 In order to follow Jesus' example of humility as indicated in the previous two questions,

what should you think of yourself?

I am a sinner, saved only by grace not merit

what should your attitude be toward others?

They deserve from me what I received from Christ

what should your actions be?

Take opp to help, encourage, support - no competition

---

7 Some people think being humble reflects weakness and allows others to exploit them. Did people take advantage of Jesus? Explain.

They thought so: time, attention, healing; whipping, cross etc

Humility is pride in God.
Austin O'Malley

"Let's go over my sermon again. Surely I must have said SOMETHING."

4. Generous

Study passage   2 Corinthians 9

Focus   2 Corinthians 9:6-7: Remember this: Whoever sows sparingly will also reap sparingly, and whoever sows generously will also reap generously. Each man should give what he has decided in his heart to give, not reluctantly or under compulsion, for God loves a cheerful giver.

The fund raising project Paul refers to in this passage is also mentioned in Romans 15:25-28 and 1 Corinthians 16:1-4. "This service to the saints" was a benefit to the Jerusalem church. Among other difficulties, they were experiencing a famine in their area. Paul actively pursued this project to bring relief to the "mother church" in Jerusalem.

1 What words and phrases in 2 Corinthians 9 refer to giving?

Service (verse 1) *12,13*
offering for the saints *contribution*
gift
giver
provide
given
generosity *11,13*

2 In encouraging the Corinthians to be generous, Paul was careful to show them how it would help everyone. What benefits are there in generous giving

for the giver? *God loves them*
reaping
enough to provide for g good work
enriched in g way
glorify God
no humiliation

resources multiplied
harvest of righteousness unmeet
glorify God
(obedience i acknowledge gospel
others pray for you
_____ for you

for the receiver?
supplies wants of _____
thats _____ to God

for others?
stirred them _____ to give
not be humiliated
Paul could boast

Considering your answers above, what motivates you to be a generous giver?

I receive > recipient
I reap as I sow
I will receive so I can give more

3 In verse 2, Paul noted that the eagerness and the generosity of the Corinthians stirred others to give. What examples of generosity have encouraged you to be more generous?

Phil Downer   Coke float + Covenant
Judy Cochran

4 Paul encouraged not only the act of giving, but also the right attitudes about giving. What attitudes should and should not accompany your giving?

Right attitudes	Wrong attitudes
Cheerful	reluctance
obedient	Compelled
ready	c convenience
liberally	
c thanksgiving	

What do you find helps you maintain right attitudes?

Keep att'n on Christ, eager to be conformed to His image, seeing I am or made by Him for Me

5 When there is generous giving with the right attitudes, God responds to you: "And God is able to make all grace abound to you" (verse 8). Considering the entire study passage, what do you think *all grace* means?

Give an example of someone experiencing all grace.

6 Generosity is encouraged throughout the Bible. Many times calls to generosity are accompanied by promises. Locate two other Bible passages that give promises to a person who is generous. Write the promises below.

2 Cor 8:2-15, 24 esp 12-15 (& 16:18)   Lk 15:7-11
& 25:2
Act 20:32-35
Pr. 28:27, 19:17, 21:13
[Pr. 30:7-9]

What is the most important lesson you learned as
you completed this study?

My highlight—

I am still not a giver

5. Submissive

Study passage 1 Peter 2:13-25

Focus 1 Peter 2:13: Submit yourselves for the Lord's sake to every authority instituted among men.

---

1 To gain an overview of the passage, write in your own words all the commands you find.

2 One of the commands you listed is, "Submit to every authority instituted among men." What reason is given for you to submit? (Verse 15)

Using your knowledge of the Bible, what are some other reasons to submit?

3 The two commands in verse 16 seem to be opposites. Study the passage and explain how a person can obey both these commands at the same time.

Live as a free man	Live as a servant

4 Submitting seems to be difficult for almost everyone. We like to express our independence. Perhaps the most difficult time to submit is during an injustice. According to the study passage, why should you be willing to suffer for doing good?

5 Jesus is our example of submitting and of suffering for doing good. What did He do (or not do) that you can imitate?

Why do you think He is such an excellent example of suffering wrongfully?

6 Choose one of the following situations and tell how you would apply the study passage.

Situation 1: You take a job at a factory and, in your desire to work heartily as to the Lord, you become the top producer. In fact, your production is almost twice the average. However, your efforts are not appreciated by the other workers because you make them look lazy. One day the foreman calls you into his office and tells you that you are the cause of unrest in the plant, and if it continues, you will be fired.

Situation 2: The church board has just canceled the Saturday morning prayer breakfast. It was the spiritual highlight of your week. You talk to them and ask that they reconsider, but without any discussion, they deny your request. The only reason they give you for canceling this program is to keep it from competing with the Sunday morning service. This doesn't make any sense to you because those who attend the prayer meeting are also at the Sunday service.

Lord, help me to see that I'm submitting to You
when I submit to those You've placed over me.

"Of course, on the other hand . . ."

6. Uncompromising

Study passage   Daniel 6

Focus   Daniel 6:10: Now when Daniel learned that the decree had been published, he went home to his upstairs room where the windows opened toward Jerusalem. Three times a day he got down on his knees and prayed, giving thanks to his God, just as he had done before.

1 The events described in this passage took place about 600 years before Christ, under the rule of Darius, the king of Babylon. It was the strongest empire up to that time and ruled the world. Much earlier, Daniel had been brought to the city of Babylon with several other young Jews to be trained in the ways of the Babylonians.

Read verses 1-5. Then describe Daniel's character and the position to which he was appointed.

2 Although Daniel acted wisely, not everyone appreciated him. How did the governors (satraps) react to him?

Describe how these men plotted against Daniel. (Verses 6-9)

3 How did Daniel show an uncompromising attitude? (Verses 10-15)

In the previous chapter, you studied submitting. Do you think Daniel could have submitted to the decree without compromising his faith? Explain.

4 According to verses 16-24, how did Daniel's uncompromising attitude affect King Darius?

What are other ways you have seen an uncompromising attitude affect people?

5 What were the results of Daniel's uncompromising action?

Stephen is another example of an uncompromising person. He refused to change his message to satisfy religious leaders of his day. What were the results of his uncompromising action? (Acts 7:54-60)

Why do you think there were such vastly different results in these two cases?

6 Review the study passage. In what ways do you view Daniel as a submissive person?

In what ways do you see that he wasn't a submissive person?

7 What are some ways people are tempted to compromise today?

How are you tempted to compromise? What can you do to prepare yourself to overcome this temptation?

Therefore, my dear brothers, stand firm. Let nothing move you. Always give yourselves fully to the work of the Lord, because you know that your labor in the Lord is not in vain.

Paul to the Corinthian church
1 Corinthians 15:58

"Come in pastor. We were expecting you."

7. Careful in Speech

Study passage   James 3:1-12

Focus   James 3:2: We all stumble in many ways. If anyone is never at fault in what he says, he is a perfect man, able to keep his whole body in check.

---

1 James uses several "pictures," such as a "bit" (verse 3) to teach about the tongue. Identify these pictures and briefly explain what characteristic of the tongue each picture presents. (Two pictures may present the same idea.)

Picture	Explanation
A bit	*a guide for the whole body*

Picture	Explanation
a rudder	guide the ship acc to will of pilot
small fire	whole forest set ablaze
a fire	
defiler	of whole body
evil	untameable

Choose one picture and give an example from your life to illustrate that point.

Coming home to find happy family in bed - complained instead of joy! I'm going to ruin it.

---

2 Verses 7 and 8 claim that, unlike many wild animals, the tongue cannot be tamed. Like a rattlesnake, it is untamable and full of poison. Imagine a rattlesnake lives in your house and you cannot kill it or move from your house. Describe how you must conduct your life.

Watchful, fearful - looking g where around before moving. Gradually becoming accustomed to it, wait for rattle to flee - stop looking

How is this similar to living with your tongue?

I am so used to talking. I don't realize how I sound or what I say. Only when I see a reaction do I know - or remember later how I must have sounded.

---

3 One of the poisons of the tongue is degrading speech. What reasons can you find in verses 9-12 for not using your tongue to degrade others?

men are made after likeness of God & ~~are object of~~

sickness or fellowship

~~our~~ all should be consistent

What other reasons can you give not to degrade others, even "in jest"?

All are to be witnessed to or love fellowship

---

4 In verse 12, James repeats a concept he probably learned from Jesus. Read Luke 6:43-45. What did Jesus say ultimately controls your speech?

*Overflow of heart
not deep, but yes superficial, unthinking
My words must be in our thoughts first, come
out of me, not put in me*

How do you think Jesus intended His followers to apply this information? *I talk like I hear – like tape mental-
good man – saved, discipled, being renewed
in mind – fruit & words are changed
from bad to good. What I am is not simp*

---

5 Considering both the James 3 and Luke 6 passages, what do you consider to be the best way for your tongue to be a constructive force in your church? *Eph 4:29*

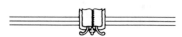

"My talent is to speak my mind," said a woman to John Wesley. "I am sure, sister," Wesley answered, "that God wouldn't object if you buried *that* talent."

"I'd like to thank the board for this lovely plant,
especially after our disagreement this week."

8. Forgiving

Study passage   Matthew 18:21-35

Focus   Matthew 18:27: The servant's master took pity on him, canceled
the debt and let him go.

---

1 The passage consists of three main parts—a principle stated,
a principle illustrated, a principle applied. Briefly explain
each part in your own words.

The principle (verses 21-22)

The illustration (verses 23-34)

The application (verse 35)

2 Jesus told Peter how often to forgive. If you believe Jesus meant this literally, tell how you can fulfill it. If you believe He meant this figuratively, tell what you think He intends for you to do.

3 To illustrate the principle of forgiveness, Jesus told a parable. Briefly describe how this parable illustrates God's forgiveness.

What does the parable teach about how you should treat other people, and why you should treat them in that way?

4 The king said the servant should cancel a fellow servant's debt because his own debt had been canceled. List some Bible verses that tell how your "debt" has been canceled.

5 Although the Bible clearly teaches unconditional forgiveness, just as Christ forgave you, people still use many arguments to justify their attitudes. What are some reasons people express for not forgiving others?

Tell how you would respond to one of these reasons, using thoughts from this passage.

6 Had the servant forgiven his fellow servant, he would have avoided a harsh punishment. What benefits do you receive when you forgive?

Benefits given in this passage

Benefits given in other Bible passages

Benefits based on your experience and knowledge

7 The principle of forgiveness being studied and illustrated is of real value only when you apply it. Take a few minutes to think through these questions:

- Do you have a strained relationship with anyone at home, at work, at church, or elsewhere?
- Would forgiveness help the relationship?
- Have you fully forgiven the other person from your heart?
- Have you expressed your forgiveness?
- Do you need to be forgiven? Have you apologized?

God,
thank You for the freedom
You give me to say,
"You're forgiven" to someone—
and mean it.

"Kind of makes a girl feel inferior, doesn't it?"

9. Pure

Study passage 1 Thessalonians 4:1-12

Focus 1 Thessalonians 4:7: For God did not call us to be impure, but to live a holy life.

1 In a day when so many consider morality to be relative, it is not enough to know that God has called you to purity. You must know His concept of purity. What characteristics of a pure person and an impure person are mentioned in this passage?

Pure person	Impure person

Pure person	Impure person

What do you conclude is God's idea of purity?

2 Words and concepts that are repeated in a passage generally are important. When concepts are repeated in different wording, they are more difficult to observe, but not less important. What fact do verses 2, 3, 8, and 9 emphasize?

Why do you think this is so important when dealing with purity?

3 How do you think the qualities described in verses 9-12 will lead to purity?

4 From what you have observed, in what ways do some Christians flirt with impurity?

5 Why should you be pure, according to the study passage?

according to other passages?

according to your experience?

6 Bill came to his pastor for help. He wanted to be pure, but he felt he was very impure. As they talked, Bill disclosed that he was not participating in sexually impure relationships, but he fantasized often about impure activities. If you were his pastor, what questions would you ask him?

What verses would you present to him?

What suggestions would you make?

More purity give me, more strength to o'ercome;
More freedom from earth-stains, more longings for home;
More fit for the kingdom, more used would I be;
More blessed and holy, more, Savior, like Thee.
Philip P. Bliss
Hymn

"Pastor, just thought we'd let you see the carpet we picked for the youth hall!"

10. Sensitive

Study passage Romans 14

Focus Romans 14:13: Therefore let us stop passing judgment on one another. Instead, make up your mind not to put any stumbling block or obstacle in your brother's way.

In this chapter you will be using a slightly different method of study. Instead of writing your answers below the questions, you'll write them next to the text that is printed for you. (The exception will be the chart in question 2.)

This will make it easier for you to relate your comments to the passage. Use your creativity in this study, marking the passage in any way that helps you study it.

If this style of studying is fun and beneficial for you, look for a wide-margin or a loose-leaf Bible that you can continue to use. Because markings may damage the pages, you may wish to buy an inexpensive one.

Romans 14

Accept him whose faith is weak, without passing judgment on disputable matters. [2]One man's faith allows him to eat everything, but another man, whose faith is weak, eats only vegetables. [3]The man who eats everything must not look down on him who does not, and the man who does not eat everything must not condemn the man who does, for God has accepted him. [4]Who are you to judge someone else's servant? To his own master he stands or falls. And he will stand, for the Lord is able to make him stand.

[5]One man considers one day more sacred than another; another man considers every day alike. Each one should be fully convinced in his own mind. [6]He who regards one day as special, does so to the Lord. He who eats meat, eats to the Lord, for he gives thanks to God; and he who abstains, does so to the Lord and gives thanks to God. [7]For none of us lives to himself alone and none of us dies to himself alone. [8]If we live, we live to the Lord, and if we die, we die to the Lord. So, whether we live or die, we belong to the Lord.

[9]For this very reason, Christ died and returned to life so that he might be the Lord of both the dead and the living. [10]You, then, why do you judge your brother? Or why do you look down on your brother? For we will all stand before God's judgment seat. [11]It is written:

"'As surely as I live,' says the Lord,
'Every knee will bow before me;
    every tongue will confess to God.'"

[12]So then, each of us will give an account of himself to God.

[13]Therefore let us stop passing judgment on one another. Instead, make up your mind not to put any stumbling block or obstacle in your brother's way. [14]As one who is in the Lord Jesus, I am fully convinced that no food is unclean in itself. But if anyone regards something as unclean, then for him it is unclean. [15]If your brother is distressed because of what you eat, you are no longer acting in love. Do not by your eating destroy your brother for whom Christ died. [16]Do not allow what you consider good to be spoken of as evil. [17]For the kingdom of God is not a matter of eating and drinking, but of righteousness, peace and joy in the Holy Spirit, [18]because anyone who serves Christ in this way is pleasing to God and approved by men.

[19]Let us therefore make every effort to do what leads to peace and to mutual edification. [20]Do not destroy the work of God for the sake of food. All food is clean, but it is wrong for a man to eat anything that causes someone else to stumble. [21]It is better not to eat meat or drink wine or to do anything else that will cause your brother to fall.

[22]So whatever you believe about these things keep between yourself and God. Blessed is the man who does not condemn him-

self by what he approves. [23]But the man who has doubts is condemned if he eats, because his eating is not from faith; and everything that does not come from faith is sin.

1 After you have read the passage several times, go through each paragraph and underline a sentence (or part of a sentence) that you feel is the focal point of the paragraph. Remember, your selections will probably be different from those of other people; there are no right or wrong answers.

2 In the first paragraph (verses 1-4), Paul talks about two kinds of people. One is called "weak." The other might be considered stronger. Compare these people in the chart below.

	Weak	Stronger
What does this person think is proper to eat?	only vegetables	everything
What command is given to this person?	do not condemn the other (one who eats everything)	do not look down on ī who eats not

Why should these commands be obeyed? (Verse 4)

Both stand or fall before the Lord only, we don't judge another servant

3 In the second paragraph (verses 5-8), Paul mentions another issue some people disagree about. What is it?

Regarding ī day more sacred or special than another; eating meat or abstaining

What is true about people on both sides of this issue or others like it?

we don't live to myself alone - I belong to God

48

Is this generally true about people who disagree about issues like these? Explain. *Yes; all such dissension disrupts unity, oneness of purpose. But, most are not Christ's — he focus on knowing him & reproducing.*

---

4 In verse 10, the commands given in verse 3 are repeated as questions. What reason for obeying these commands is given in this paragraph? (Verses 9-12) *each of us will give account of himself to God*

---

5 Instead of insisting upon being recognized as right or judging the other person, what does a sensitive person do? (Verses 13-18) *Stops judging & putting an obstacle in a brother's way.*

---

6 Verse 20 says it is wrong to do something "that causes someone else to stumble." What does it mean to cause someone to stumble? *to stop progress in the "way"; to deviate off course; to leave the fellowship; to defend himself & become more self-centered*

Give an example of how one person could cause another person to stumble. *Dumas — diet/wk/Shahlee became part of testimony, they began to criticize others, giving unwanted advice, applying pressure (even to buy what they were selling) End — working in Burger King; leaving town.*

7 Tell one way you can apply the teaching of this passage to become more sensitive to others.

I belong to the Lord — He is my Master and I must answer & give account to Him — so I " keep quiet about <u>non essential differences</u> *& make every effort to promote peace & mutual edification. Also think, consider, pray through, seek word about all I do — all must be from Faith.*

disputable matters

In essentials—unity,
In nonessentials—liberty,
In all things—charity.
Philipp Melancthon

"Last night John really showed me he loves me.
He promised to give up his motorcycle."

11. A Good Family Member

Study passage   Ephesians 5:15-6:4

Focus   Ephesians 5:17: Therefore do not be foolish, but understand what the Lord's will is.

---

1 When studying a passage with a specific focus (such as family relationships), it is easy to overlook general statements that also apply to this focus. For example, "Be very careful, then, how you live" is as important for family life as for any other area of living. This study passage begins at verse 15 with this admonition because verses 15-21 have general commands that are basic to good family relationships.

Choose one command in this paragraph and tell how obeying

it can improve family relationships or how ignoring it can destroy them.

2 Completing the following chart will help you gain an overview of this passage.

Who is addressed	Command	Reason for command (if given)	Verses
			5:22-24
			5:25-33
			6:1-3
			6:4

3 God builds families on the foundation of marriage. Paul says the relationship between husbands and wives is similar to the relationship between Christ and the Church. List as many similarities as possible, using both the passage and your ideas.

4 Contemporary studies indicate that major problems in marriage center around (1) money, (2) in-laws, and (3) children. How do you think this model for marriage can help people in these areas?

Money	In-laws	Children

5 A healthy husband-wife relationship is only one part of being a good family member. Paul quotes Moses: "Honor your father and mother!" Based on the passage and your ideas, how can children honor their parents?

How do you think adults can honor their parents?

54

6 Fathers are told not to exasperate their children. What are some things that exasperate children?

Give your explanation of how to avoid exasperating children by "the training and instruction of the Lord" (6:4).

7 In one sense, your church is also a family. God is your Father, and you are all sisters and brothers. How will the teachings of this passage help you improve these relationships?

A light that does not shine beautifully around the family table at home is not fit to rush . . . off to do a great service elsewhere.

Hudson Taylor

"The sopranos and altos will sing 'Hallelujah,' the tenors will sing 'Amen,' and the basses will sing 'Oo-wah, diddle-dee, doo-wah.'"

12. Worshipful

Study passage   Psalm 145

Focus   Psalm 145:3: Great is the LORD and most worthy of praise; his greatness no one can fathom.

---

1 God should be praised both for *who* He is and *what* He does. "Holy, holy, holy! Lord God Almighty!" is the beginning of a hymn praising God for His righteousness. Another hymn begins, "I sing the mighty power of God, that made the mountains rise; that spread the flowing seas abroad, and built the lofty skies."

Psalm 145 is a song of praise to God. In the chart on the next page, write at least three things found in the passage that tell who God is and three more that tell what He does. Then make a personal application for each statement.

God is	What this means to me
Great (verse 3)	Praiseworthy
1.	
2.	
3.	

God does	One way I have experienced this
He holds me up (verse 14).	He brought me through the trial of my mother dying.
1.	
2.	
3.	

2 One of the main activities associated with worship is praise. What is praise?

How do *you* praise God?

What parts of your church service of worship are focused toward praising God?

3 What activities of worship, in addition to praise, are mentioned in this passage?

Explain how you include these activities in your church services.

4 Verse 5 says, "I will meditate on your wonderful works." Spend some time meditating on things God has done in and for you. Then record your thoughts about God below.

After meditating upon God's works, David said, "I will proclaim your great deeds" (verse 6). How can you follow David's example?

5 Find a place to be alone and read this psalm to God aloud. Read it slowly and prayerfully. Be ready to tell your group how this exercise affected you spiritually and emotionally.

I worship You, O God, for all Your mighty works. The sun, moon, and stars remind me of Your celestial power. But at times Your quiet and steady work in me seems just as amazing. You've made me different. There are times I'm startled by my own actions. I think, "Did I do that? That's not like me!" Then I'm reminded that You are in me, changing me into Your image.

Thank You. I love You!

Developing Lifelong Study Skills

The variety of methods you followed to complete the study are skills you can use throughout your life to understand and apply other passages in the Bible.

This summary identifies a few of the skills covered in this book, and will serve as a helpful guide for your future Bible study.

1. APPLYING A PRINCIPLE. For many issues, the Bible does not make a definitive statement, but instead indicates principles to apply. When you study a passage, look for underlying principles that can help you in life. One example of applying a principle occurred in chapter 1, questions 2 and 3, where you used the principle of exchange to become renewed.

2. REORGANIZING. Sometimes the same information put in a reorganized form will have a different impact on you. In chapter 2, you reorganized the statements on love from 1 Corinthians 13. You can use this method when studying other passages by making a list of two to five subtopics and then recording what the passage says about each.

3. CLAIMING PROMISES. Whenever God makes a statement about what could be true in your life, you can consider it a promise. Even when circumstances seem to indicate the opposite is true, you should cling to God's Word, expecting it to be fulfilled. In chapter 4, you listed the benefits of generous giving for the giver, the receiver, and others. These are promises you can depend upon.

4. OUTLINING. An outline can help you organize information for clearer understanding. In chapter 8, question 1, you completed an outline for the passage. When outlining a Bible passage, focus on understanding what it says rather than on constructing a technically accurate outline. It is better to enjoy your study of God's Word and to apply it to your life than to have well-constructed outlines.

5. INDIVIDUALIZING. Although biblical doctrine is objective truth, your reaction to truth is often subjective and individual. It is good to individualize the Scriptures as long as you realize you are expressing only your response and not a doctrine that would apply to others. One example of proper individualizing is in chapter 12, where you listed what the passage said about God and what God does. Then you wrote out how this affected you individually.

What Others Say

The ministry of Churches Alive is helping churches, both small and large, of more than 45 denominations to develop the resources entrusted to them by God. As churches improve their stewardship of the gifts God has given them, they convert Christians from residents to laborers in the harvest fields. Here is what church leaders are saying about the ministry of Churches Alive:

"The Churches Alive Growing by Discipling concept has been one of the most positive and fruitful endeavors we have had in Trinity Church."

DR. ROBERT J. OSTENSON
TRINITY PRESBYTERIAN CHURCH
MONTGOMERY, AL

"Churches Alive provides the vehicle by which we are successfully discipling men and women."

DR. WILLIAM C. MASON
ASBURY UNITED METHODIST CHURCH
TULSA, OK

"Discovery classes, growth groups, evangelism groups, and others have permeated every facet of our community life in Christ and are showing remarkable results."

REV. DONIS PATTERSON
BISHOP OF THE DALLAS DIOCESE
OF THE EPISCOPAL CHURCH

"I'm more convinced than ever that Churches Alive is a sound biblical program greatly needed by our churches."

REV. MAYNARD NELSON
CALVARY LUTHERAN CHURCH
GOLDEN VALLEY, MN

"Churches Alive is effectively helping our church in critical growth areas through varied discipleship approaches and encouragement and support from our Churches Alive consultant."

DR. RICHARD L. DETRICH
FAITH COMMUNITY CHURCH
(REFORMED CHURCH IN AMERICA)
LITTLETON, CO

"The growth group, with the mature leader, is invaluable in providing care and growth opportunities to a greater number of people than I could individually."

REV. JOHN W. PETERSON
VALLEY COMMUNITY BAPTIST CHURCH
AVON, CT

"Our church has been revolutionized by the Churches Alive process. Growing by Discipling has rejuvenated a dying church and transformed it into an equipping center."

REV. RICHARD ANDERSON
FIRST UNITED PRESBYTERIAN CHURCH
BELVIDERE, IL

"Your materials outshine everything I have seen."

REV. DOUG QUENZER
FRIENDSHIP CHURCH
MONDOVI, WI

"Churches Alive has placed well-designed tools into the hands of the local church."

DR. WALLACE WILSON
HIGHLANDS COMMUNITY CHURCH
RENTON, WA

Churches Alive is ready to help your church benefit from Growing by Discipling with the same helps these pastors have received. Our wide range of consulting, conference, and materials services enable you to proceed with the guidance of our gifted field staff or through a do-it-yourself approach. For more information without cost or obligation, write or call

Churches Alive International
Box 3800
San Bernardino, CA 92413
(714) 886-5361

OVERVIEW OF THE
God in You
SERIES

The book you hold in your hands is one of six in the *God in You Bible Study Series*. Each book complements the others as you explore the many privileges of God in you.

JESUS! God in You Made Possible

Immanuel	Luke 2:1-20
The Word	John 1:1-18
Savior	John 3:1-21
Friend of Sinners	John 4:4-26
Master	Matthew 8:23-9:8
Christ	Matthew 16:13-28
Servant	John 13:1-17
Bread of Life	Mark 14:12-42
Great High Priest	John 17
Man of Sorrows	John 19:16-30
Lord God Omnipotent	Luke 24
King of Kings	Acts 1:1-11

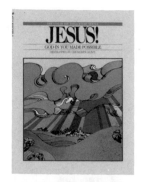

ALIVE! God in Intimate Relationship with You

Giving New Life	2 Corinthians 5:11-21
Lighting Your Way	1 John 1:1-10
Residing in You	Romans 8:5-17
Providing Fullness	Colossians 2:6-17
Granting You Access	Hebrews 4:12-16
Giving You Guidance	John 16:5-15
Being Your Companion	Psalm 27
Assuring Your Triumph	Romans 8:28-39
Reviving by His Word	Psalm 19:7-11
Responding to Your Prayers	Matthew 6:5-15
Meriting Your Trust	Psalm 37:1-11
Sustaining Your Life	John 15:1-17

RICH! God Meeting Your Deepest Needs

Love	1 John 4:7-21
Grace	Ephesians 2:1-10
Peace	Philippians 4:1-9
Acceptance	Luke 15:11-32
Clear Conscience	Hebrews 10:1-14
Wisdom	Proverbs 2
Comfort	2 Corinthians 1:3-11
Freedom	Galatians 5:1-18
Provision	Matthew 6:19-34
Family	Acts 2:41-47
Courage	Matthew 14:22-33
Hope	1 Thessalonians 4:13-5:11

POWERFUL! God Enabling You

CHANGED! Reflecting Your Love for God

FULFILLED! Enjoying God's Purpose for You

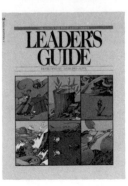

LEADER'S GUIDE

The *God in You Leader's Guide* gives help for every chapter in the series, including brief background information related to each Scripture passage, additional group discussion questions, and suggestions for the leader that will make the small group experience most helpful to the members.

FOR A FREE CATALOG OF
NAVPRESS BOOKS & BIBLE STUDIES,
CALL TOLL FREE 800-366-7788 (USA)
or 1-416-499-4615 (CANADA)